LETTERS HOME from INDIA

Marcia S. Gresko

BLACKBIRCH PRESS, INC.
WOODBRIDGE, CONNECTICUT

Published by Blackbirch Press, Inc.
260 Amity Road
Woodbridge, CT 06525

©1999 by Blackbirch Press, Inc.
First Edition

e-mail: staff@blackbirch.com
Web site: www.blackbirch.com

Printed in Singapore

10 9 8 7 6 5 4 3 2 1

Photo Credits
Cover: ©Corel Corporation, inset ©Air-India; title page: ©Air-India; pages 4, 6, 9, 10, 11, 15-19, 20 (left), 23–27, 28 (left), 29, 30: ©Corel Corporation; pages 7, 8, 12–14, 20 (right), 21, 22, 28 (right): ©Air-India.

Library of Congress Cataloging-in-Publication Data

Gresko, Marcia S.
India / by Marcia S. Gresko
    p.   cm. — (Letters Home From—)
   Summary: Describes some of the sights and experiences on a trip through India, including visits to New Delhi, the Taj Mahal, Madras, Kerala, Bombay, Rajasthan, and the Ganges.
   ISBN 1-56711-403-2
   1. India—Description and travel—Juvenile literature. 2. Gresko, Marcia S.—Journeys—India—Juvenile literature. [1. India—Description and travel.] I. Title. II. Series.
DS414.2.G76 1999   99-22795
915.404'52—dc21   CIP
                                                          AC

TABLE OF CONTENTS

Arrival in . . .

New Delhi

After flying halfway around the world, we arrived in New Delhi. That's the capital of India. The long plane ride gave me plenty of time to read about all the amazing things we're going to see!

India is a big country! It's the seventh-largest in the world and has all kinds of scenery. It has a burning desert, steamy jungles, mighty rivers, rolling plains, and the tallest mountains in the world. But, there are only two main seasons—monsoon (wet) and dry!

India also has the second-largest population in the world. Nearly a billion people live here. They come from many cultures. And they speak more than a dozen major languages.

New Delhi's modern airport was really busy. Good thing our tour guide was wearing a bright, flowing sari (body wrap) or I would have lost her before we made it to the bus!

Delhi

Visiting Delhi is really like visiting two cities at the same time!

New Delhi is a nice place. It was built by the English. India was once an English colony. New Delhi has wide, tree-lined streets, lovely gardens and parks, and really cool shops. India's Presidential Mansion and its Parliament Building, where the country's laws are made, are also here.

Old Delhi is noisy and crowded, but it's also packed with history. There are more than 1,000 ruins and monuments to explore here. Old Delhi's most famous buildings were built by Shah Jahan. He was the Muslim emperor who built the Taj Mahal (we're going to see that tomorrow!).

Delhi man

Women at the Laksminarian Temple

Jama Masjid

Rickshaws

Shah Jahan also built the Jama Masjid, India's largest Muslim temple. Before entering, our guide reminded us to take off our shoes as a sign of respect. She explained that Muslims are followers of Islam. That's the second-biggest religion in India (Hindu is the biggest). Muslims study a holy book called the Koran and pray to the god Allah.

Old Delhi has some really busy bazaars (open-air markets). Our rickshaw wove in and out between sleeping cows, sidewalk barbers and dentists, and street vendors selling everything from tea to turbans!

Agra/Taj Mahal

Yesterday we took the train 120 miles south to the city of Agra. That's where the Taj Mahal is—India's most famous sight.

We got there at dawn. As the rising sun turned the Taj Mahal's white marble a rosy pink, our guide told us the love story behind the building. The Taj Mahal was built more than 350 years ago by Shah Jahan. It was built as a tomb and monument for his favorite wife. Before she died, she asked him to build a monument so beautiful that the world would never forget their love. He began building the Taj Mahal that year.

Taj Mahal

Taj Mahal

Villagers between Agra and Jaipur

Gleaming, white marble was brought to the site by a caravan of 1,000 elephants. Precious stones were gathered from all over the world. Twenty-thousand workers labored for more than 21 years to complete the building.

The monument sits on a raised, marble platform. It is surrounded by four towers, each taller than a ten-story building. Delicate flower mosaics decorate the walls inside and out. Legend says that Shah Jahan originally planned to build a black marble copy of the Taj Mahal for his own tomb, but both he and his wife are buried here together.

Ganges

From Agra, we traveled over 300 miles southeast to the city of Varanasi. This is on the west bank of the Ganges River. It is the religious capital of Hinduism.

Our guide explained that more than three quarters of Indians are Hindu. Hindus worship many gods and goddesses. Shiva, Brahma, and Vishnu are Hinduism's most important gods. Lakshmi and Parvati are the most important goddesses. Hindus also believe that a person's soul is reborn into another body after death (that's called reincarnation).

Before sunrise we joined the crowds streaming toward the ghats, or steps, leading down to the river. Hindus consider all rivers holy, but the Ganges is

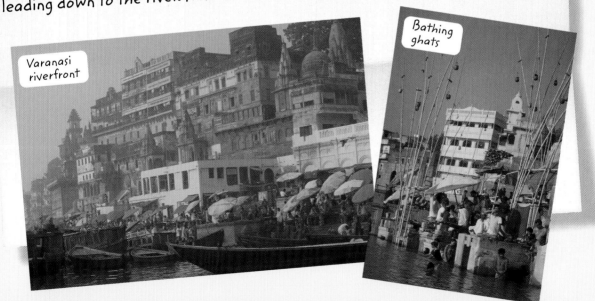

Varanasi riverfront

Bathing ghats

Sadhu
holy man

Hindu priest
making offerings

holiest of all. Rising in the Himalayas, the Ganges travels 1,500 miles across India. It finally empties into the Bay of Bengal. The river provides irrigation to the nearby farmland. It's also a major source of transportation for goods and people. It is so important that Indians call it "Mother Ganges" and consider it a goddess. They believe bathing in the Ganges washes away all your sins.

At the river, thousands of worshippers bathed and prayed. Painted Sadhus (holy men) practiced yoga, or washed their tattered clothes. All along the water, you can see flickering oil lamps and fragrant flowers. These are offerings to the goddess, Mother Ganges.

Calcutta

Today we traveled southeast from Varanasi to Calcutta. We took India's most popular form of transportation—the train. India has the fourth-largest railroad system in the world. Even so, there are still plenty of elephants, camels, and bullock-drawn carts on the country roads!

Calcutta is India's third-largest city. Our tour guide said it's named after the fierce Indian goddess, Kali.

There's always something happening on the streets of Calcutta. In busy bazaars, vendors sell their wares. Snake charmers do their shows for the tourists, and fortune-tellers predict the future. But Calcutta was not all fun

Old Calcutta

Fruit vendors

Crowded market

White tiger

Bengal tiger

and games. There are thousands of poor and homeless people on the streets. Our guide said that most of these people don't have electricity, running water, or toilets.

India is an incredible place for seeing wild animals. Less than 100 miles outside Calcutta is the largest natural habitat of tigers in the world! About 2,000 kinds of birds and 500 kinds of mammals live in India. There are elephants, rhinoceroses, bears, antelope, monkeys, leopards, wild goats, and sheep. It's a good thing the government has set up many wildlife preserves and parks to protect India's amazing variety of animals.

13

Madras

Yesterday we took an 850-mile-flight south from Calcutta to Madras. This took us from northern to southern India.

Southern India is mostly a huge, rocky plateau. It is separated from the rest of the country by mountains. As a result, its native Dravidian culture has changed very little in 5,000 years. Proud Dravidians still speak four ancient languages and have a rich collection of poetry and literature. They have their own style of architecture and observe many of their own unique traditions.

We're staying in Madras. It's India's fourth-largest city. It's also the capital of Tamil Nadu, India's most southern state. Like most of the south, Madras has a warm, tropical climate.

Sadhu, Madras

Madras City

14

Shiva Temple, Madras

Madras High Court

It's hard to believe that bustling Madras was once a small, coastal fishing village. It became a major trading port when the English built a fort here. Many of the grand buildings that house the city's offices, museums, and galleries were built by the English. The huge High Court is the second-largest court building in the world!

Tamil Nadu

We spent the last two days exploring the southern countryside between Madras and the city of Madurai.

One thing's for certain: we sure are lucky living where we do! You should see the rural villages here. Homes are made of mud and straw. There's some electricity, but few homes have running water. Nearby wells and streams are busy places. Most villages have a small, simple school-house that children attend, but only when they are not working.

Members of the village families help each other. Families here are large and close. Relatives often live together and farm the family's nearby fields. Making jewelry and weaving also provide jobs for millions of village workers.

Mango stall, Madurai

Bullock Festival in Madurai

Village jewelry

We traveled a lot by bus, rolling past fields of sugarcane, cotton, nuts, tea, and spices. And lots of rice. That's India's most widespread and important crop. It's easy to see that farming methods have changed very little over the centuries. Farmers still use cattle and water buffalo for plowing. Cattle are considered sacred, and strict Hindus are vegetarians.

Wow! I tried some spicy vegetable curry, or stew, last night. It takes a while to get used to it! So does using your fingers and chappati (flat bread) to scoop it all up!

Tamil Nadu

Legend says that the city of Madurai was formed from a single drop of water shaken from the Hindu god Shiva's hair! Madurai is also called the "city of festivals." A major festival is celebrated eleven months out of the year. Indian festivals are times for family and friends to visit, eat, and observe religious rituals. Parades, fairs, street entertainment, and dancing are all part of the fun.

Madurai's centuries-old streets are laid out like India's national flower—the lotus. The Minakshi Temple is in the center of the city. It's huge! It's dedicated to Shiva and Minakshi, his companion. Four nine-story-high

Priest with village deities

Village deity, Tamil Nadu

Tower of Minakshi Temple

gopurams, or entrance towers, guard the walls surrounding it. Believers stream into the temple nearly all day long to make offerings. They perform puja, or worship, in front of their gods.

In the cool evening hours, you can listen to temple musicians play traditional music. They play stringed instruments, cymbals, flutes, and gongs. When we went, the highlight of the evening was watching the temple's closing ceremony. A procession carried a statue of Shiva to Minakshi's shrine to sleep by her side. A Hindu priest explained that the statue is returned to its own shrine the next morning.

Kerala

This morning we traveled about 130 miles from Madurai to Cochin on the coast of the southwestern state of Kerala.

Traders from Europe, the Middle East, and China have been visiting Kerala for thousands of years. It's the land of spices that Columbus was searching for when he accidently discovered the Americas!

Cochin, where we are staying, is a port city. It sits on a cluster of islands in the Arabian Sea. The port is clogged with ships carrying coconuts and cashew nuts, tea and spices, rice, and rubber grown on Kerala's farms.

Bullock and cart, Kottayam

Peanut vendors

Monkey

Girl with flowers in her hair

One morning we boarded a long, low, dugout boat. Our guide took us through a maze of inland waterways. Fishing is an important way of life here and in other cities. India has more than 4,350 miles of coastline.

The highlight of our stay was a really cool performance of Kathakali dance. Kerala is famous for it. The name means "story play," and dancers in heavy make-up and fancy costumes act out ancient tales about gods and heroes. The mostly male dancers train for many years. They practice the complicated movements and facial expressions that tell the stories. Dance is one of India's richest art forms.

Bombay

This afternoon, we flew from Cochin—about 650 miles north—to Bombay. This is India's largest city.

According to the guidebook, 300 years ago Bombay was a small trading post belonging to the country of Portugal. When the King of England married a Portuguese princess, he received the city as a wedding gift!

As Bombay grew, it became known as the "gateway to India." That's because most of the trade between Europe and India came through the city's large, deep harbor. Located on an island off India's western coast, Bombay is still the country's chief port. It is also India's center for business and industry. Factories here manufacture everything from cars and chemicals to canned foods and cotton textiles. Textile manufacturing is India's most important industry.

Bombay

Bombay

Merry-go-round, seaside, Bombay

Camel rides, seaside, Bombay

Touring Bombay was a lot like visiting any large, modern city. Skyscrapers, high-rise hotels, and modern apartment towers line the avenues. Wealthy families live in large, air-conditioned homes and drive fancy cars. But, as in Calcutta, there are also large, crowded slums.

No matter what part of busy Bombay we visited, there were movie posters everywhere! More movies are made here than anywhere else in the world! That's why Bombay is nicknamed "Bollywood."

Rajasthan and the Thar Desert

When we got here, I couldn't believe it! Rajasthan is like a different country! It's India's second-largest state. And it has many different landscapes. There are fairytale cities and rugged hills, sparkling lakes—even golden sand dunes. Rajasthan means "land of the rajahs" or kings. The state was once made up of more than 20 separate kingdoms. The fierce warrior princes who ruled them often fought one another, as well as invaders from the north.

Our hotel in Udaipur is on an island in the middle of a beautiful lake. It was once a great palace, and we imagined we were part of the court of a rich king!

Jain architecture, Thar Desert

Jain priests

Lake Palace, former Maharaja's Palace

Camel driver and camel, Thar Desert

Sand dunes, Thar Desert

At the Jain temple in Ranakpur, we had to leave everything made of leather outside. Our guide explained that Jainism teaches that all life is sacred. Strict Jains may even cover their mouths with cloths to prevent accidentally swallowing bugs.

The desert city of Jaisalmer looks like a giant sandcastle! It has an 800-year-old fort and narrow, winding streets that lead to temples, palaces, and magnificent stone mansions. We took a camel safari to Thar Desert National Park. Thar means "home of death." I guess it was named that because it's such a harsh place to live.

Jaipur

Our visit to eastern Rajasthan was divided into stays in two cities.
Jaipur is the capital of Rajasthan. It is called the "pink city." According to the guidebook, the ancient walled city was painted pink, the color of welcome, to honor a visiting English prince.

At the grand City Palace, we got a look at what the luxurious lifestyle of a maharajah must have been like. Every room held treasures—paintings, sculptures, carpets, and costumes. An armory displayed the warrior family's guns, swords, and other weapons. Nearby, was the Palace of the Winds. Behind its lacy stone screens, the king's many wives could look out on the passing scenery.

Jaipur

Jaipur, sunset over Mosque

Potter, Jaipur

Sacred Pushkar Lake, Rajasthan

One afternoon, we poked through Jaipur's busy, spice-scented street bazaars. We discovered some of the beautiful items that Rajasthani craftsworkers have been making for centuries—enamelware, textiles, the region's unusual blue pottery, and fancy stonework.

Like millions of Hindus, we also made a pilgrimage to the holy city of Pushkar. Legend tells that lovely Pushkar Lake was formed where the god Brahma dropped a lotus flower. Hindus come to bathe in the lake's holy waters, which they believe are second in power after those of the sacred Ganges.

Kashmir

We weren't sure we would be able to travel to this northwestern state until we got here! This is one of the most beautiful areas of India, but it has been a battleground for the last ten years. Both India and Pakistan (India's neighbor to the west) claim it. Sadly, there's a lot of fighting here and travel is limited.

Like most visitors to Kashmir, we're staying on one of the thousand houseboats on Dal Lake. The lake is a watery neighborhood! The owner of our boat lives on another one nearby.

Boatload of crops
on Dal Lake

Himalayas, Mt.
Kanchenjunga

Festival boat
on Dal Lake

Canals of
Dal Lake

Vegetable merchant,
Dal Lake

Long boats called shikaras are used for everything from floating supermarkets to taxis. Shikara shops are stocked with traditional Kashmiri crafts—carpets, shawls, and fancy papier mache boxes. They paddled up right alongside our houseboat to display their wares!

From the rooftop deck of our houseboat, we had an awesome view of the Himalayas. They're incredible! The Himalayas are the oldest and tallest mountains in the world. As the sun set, I hoped that Kashmir's troubles would end soon so more people could enjoy this lovely land.

Leh, Ladakh

Our short flight east to Kashmir's Ladakh region took us right over the snowy Himalaya Mountains. What a sight! We're staying in Ladakh's ancient capital city of Leh.

The clifftop Leh Palace was once the home of the region's royal family. From there, Ladakh looks like another world! One of its nicknames is "moonland" because of its harsh desert landscape.

Another nickname for Leh is "Little Tibet." That's because people follow traditions similar to the people of Tibet, a region in nearby China. Many follow the Buddhist religion. Buddhism was founded in India more than 2,000 years ago.

Temple of Leh Palace, Ladakh

Harvest season, Indus Valley

Ladakhi woman

Monasteries are the center of life. An early morning jeep ride to the Thikse monastery got us there in time to see the monks perform the sunrise religious rituals. From Thikse, we went to the Hemis monastery to enjoy a grand festival honoring an important Buddhist teacher. Red-robed monks in tall hats played drums, cymbals, and ten-foot-long trumpets. Monks dressed as gods and demons performed sacred dances and acted out really cool stories from Buddhist history.

Glossary

Bazaar a street market.

Climate the usual weather of an area.

Court the home, family, and friends of a king, queen, or ruler.

Maharajah a Hindu prince.

Monastery a group of buildings where monks live and work.

Monsoon the rainy summer season in some countries.

Mosaic a pattern or picture made up of pieces of colored glass, tile, or stone.

Plateau an area of high flat land.

Rickshaw a small carriage with two wheels and a cover that is usually pulled by one person.

Rural to do with the countryside, or a less-populated area.

Slum overcrowded, poor, and neglected area of housing in a town or city.

For More Information

Books

Bailey, Donna. Malcom Rodgers. *India* (Where We Live). Chatham, NJ: Steck-Vaughn Library Division, 1990.

Denny, Roz. *A Taste of India* (Food Around the World). Chatham, NJ: Raintree/Steck Vaughn, 1994.

Hermes, Jules M. *The Children of India* (The World's Children). Minneapolis, MN: Carolrhoda Books, 1993.

Kagda, Falaq. Elizabeth Berg (Editor). *India* (Festivals Around the World). Milwaukee, WI: Gareth Stevens, 1997.

Video

Discovery Channel Home Video. *Wild India*.

Web Site
I Love India!

Play the jukebox to listen to some Indian music, or watch the slide show to see 200 beautiful places within the country—www.iloveindia.com.

Index